WITHDRAWN

THE EASTERN EUROPE COLLECTION

ADVISORY EDITOR: **HARRY SCHWARTZ**
Soviet Affairs Specialist
  The New York Times Editorial Board
University Professor
  State University College, New Paltz, New York

MASARYK'S PATH AND LEGACY

Edvard Beneš

ARNO PRESS & THE NEW YORK TIMES
New York · 1971

Reprint Edition 1971 by Arno Press Inc.

LC# 77-135793

ISBN 0-405-02735-4

The Eastern Europe Collection
ISBN for complete set 0-405-02730-3

Manufactured in the United States of America

DB
217
.m3
B43
1971

21ST SEPTEMBER 1937

Dr. Edvard Beneš
PRESIDENT OF THE CZECHOSLOVAK REPUBLIC

Masaryk's Path and Legacy

FUNERAL ORATION AT THE BURIAL OF THE
President-Liberator

21. SEPTEMBER 1937

T. G. Masaryk.

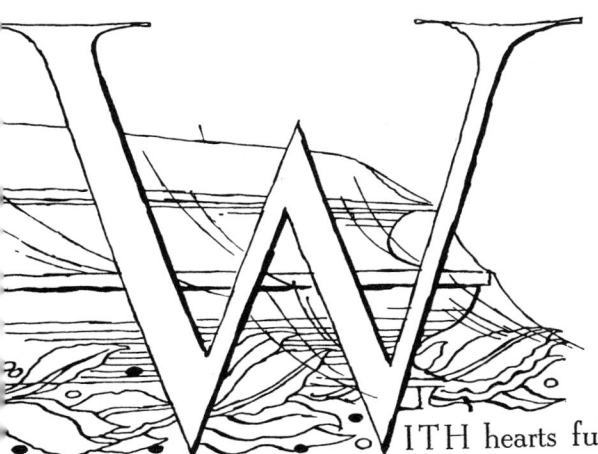

WITH hearts full of emotion and grief we stand here before the coffin of our great Dead. As we think of that great life, a life so abundantly full, a life which covered nearly a whole century, we think of the amazing wealth of intellectual work and of achievement that it represented, we reflect upon the sense of that great life's pilgrimage, and slowly into our hearts there enters calm, clarity, certainty, firmnes, and pride.

And how can we be other than calm, and firm when we look upon the clear and straight path which that life shows us? How be other than full of pride, pious and dignified pride, when we see that this nation and State possesses, and gives to itself and others, to our time and the contemporary world, a man who is one of those great guides in life such as Providence gives nation and mankind only once in whole centuries!

Eighty-seven years of a completely full life, more than sixty of which he devoted to a struggle for the comprehension of man;

reflected how to master the metaphysical problem of life and the world, how to interpret all the questions of spiritual, intellectual, political and social life; for more than fifty years sought how to triumph over all the difficulties of the practical life of a nation and daily organize and lead the State, how to attain practical knowledge of self, of nation, of State, of Europe, of all other nations and their problems; and at the same time he daily entered upon grave political struggles in concrete questions and undertook all the detailed work of political practice, first within his own nation, afterwards in the old Empire, in the European crisis and the Great War, and then founded and consolidated the State, and all the time steadily prepared for us who are left behind a legacy, and paths along which it now falls to us to carry Masaryk's torch, the torch which so splendidly shone forth into the world!

Such, in brief, was the life of Masaryk. His journey round the world during the Great War—at the most tragic movement in the evolution of the modern world when all the problems of contemporary man were, so to say, concentrated in the struggle of four terrible years—is a symbol of his activities in the realm of thought and politics, and of his broad-based universal character.

In the Eighties of last century he came to Prague University and in the first twenty years or so of his activities as man of learning, philosopher, cultural and social "awakener" and pioneer, he linked up our national and cultural development, till then very provincial, with world development. He stirred up our national world, made it uneasy with itself, influenced and fertilized it with all the problems of the life and the world of that day. He posed the problem of religion to the individual, and annihilated the religious liberalism and indifference existing among us; he extended our young philosophy and learning, till then living in a German environment, to the field of Western Europe and the whole world. He led our romantic Slavdom to practical and realist paths determined by facts; with admirable vigour he brought our local patriotism to European and world horizons; our local disputes in daily politics, in the field of art, of literature and learning he placed under the strong rays of the light of European and world criticism—it is enough to recall, for example, his struggles that centred round the conception of patriotism, his fight against cultural eclecticism, the battles he fought in the matter of the Manuscripts, ritual superstition, the sense of Czech history and Church and religious questions—he posed our social and labour problem to our middle classes within the framework of the social change in Europe and the world in the nineteenth and twentieth centuries and from the angle of philosophical-sociological criticism of the then official socialist doctrine.

In a word, *he completed the ideological, intellectual and cultural re-birth of our nation.* Masaryk was our last national, spiritual and moral pioneer and "awakener". He was the last and the greatest in that he crowned the intellectual awakening by political and constitutional re-birth, and—as a Moravian Slovak— by Czechoslovak unity. From the beginning of the sixteenth century Bohemia was in decline and not until the close of the eighteenth century did slight signs of re-birth appear. The World War and our revolt represents the final stage of this upward historical trend. *It was Masaryk who achieved our recovery and our definitive victory.*

From the Nineties of last century he entered the field of practical politics. He always gave philosophy and learning a practical aim—truth in thought and in science and learning was to be sought so that it might be applied to daily life. In the practical politics of the day he set himself his first and fundamental problem—that of the position of the reborn nation in the old Empire and in Europe. In order to discover the right path for further advance and for his struggle for cultural and political freedom he examined first of all its philosophy of history. In order to assess rightly the position of the old Monarchy he examined the whole problem of Europe and the problem of the cultural, political and social evolution of the world, particularly in the past two centuries. Thus Masaryk from the Nineties became in his own person *an incorporation and concentration of the nineteenth and twentieth centuries with their grievances, with their problems and with their development.*

The French Revolution is the landmark from which dates the disintegration of mediaeval Europe. Beginning with Rene Descartes modern rationalist France came into being, and from there enlightenment and rationalist philosophy found their way to the rest of Europe. They overthrew the whole world of the classicism of the eighteenth century through the development of the natural sciences, and the sciences generally formulated the theory of progress and development and the whole philosophy of the French revolution—the idea of human equality, the rights of man and of the citizen, the idea of freedom, the humanitarian idea of international brotherhood, and finally the whole ideology of modern democracy.

Masaryk thinking of his nation, of Central Europe, of Europe and the world in the second epoch of his career, continually returns to this starting-point of modern Europe and to these bases of the nineteenth and twentieth century, systematically associating them with the evolution of English civilisation and the American Revolution.

Out of the system of enlightenment grew the modern man. Modern individualism in philosophy was co-created by the literary, artistic, social and political romanticism of the early nineteenth century and grew with them. Montesquieu and Rousseau, Washington and Lincoln, are equally the incorporation of their day and creators of new eras as were Victor Hugo and Byron, Goethe and Pushkin. The struggle against the remnants of aristocratism and theocratism and against pre-revolution anti-democracy generally which manifested itself in revolutions in France in the year 1830, in the romantic social movement round about that year in England, in the first struggles for liberalism in Germany and in the dekabrist movement in Russia was an expression of advancing intellectual, political and social revolution in the whole of Europe. The Revolution of the year 1848 was, in its entire romanticism, the political and social culmination of the epoch of romantic struggle for a new post-revolution being, a struggle which culminated in the course of the nineteenth century in the triumph of the middle-class and the so-called middle-class civilisation. The great French Revolution and its ideology also signified the triumph of the national idea, which in its modern form could only find due expression when the system of mediaeval castes had fallen; when into cultural and political life there came the first popular element, which rapidly developed and crystallized into a whole national culture. The nationality idea in its modern garb generally is a splendid flower of individualism and romanticism issuing from the enlightenment era and the French Revolution.

Individualism and romanticism issuing from the French Revolution was the humanism of the nineteenth century and a preparation for the birth of European political democracy, led by a constitutional and parliamentary middle-class which up to the end of the nineteenth century politically dominated and led liberal Europe. It gave the nineteenth century its special character and signified a new world compared with the Europe prior to the year 1789.

Examining between the years 1880 and 1900 the tasks and the possibilities of development of his nation, Masaryk followed this great intellectual, social and political struggle of the European world. He reflected, he experienced personally, and, so to say, lived through the entire problem involved in these events and in the whole intellectual development of Europe. He saw the first beginnings of European democracy, linking up as they did to the traditions of the progressing Anglo-Saxon and American democracy, he saw the rise, the growth and the evolution of political and economic Liberalism in the Thirties of the nineteenth century and noted well how in the Revolution of 1848 the first germs of the new reorientation of this great political epoch manifested themselves in the arrival of the problems of social revolution. He strove to ascertain with precision whither this new orientation tended, what was the sense and the trend of modern liberalism, capitalism and the socialism of the nineteenth century and of the scientific socialism of Marx, and above all, *what the newly emerging democracy was, and should be, for our society, our nation, for Europe and the world.*

He came to the conclusion that after the triumph of the Third estate in the course of the nineteenth century, and after the stabilization and strengthening of national cultures and national

States in Europe, a *Fourth Estate* would in every State and nation come forward to claim a share in the power and new and better conditions of existence—the estate of the worker, the farmer, the small and the middle-class manual and mental worker—that it was a vital question for the whole political society of the nineteenth century, that despite the rivalries of the Great Powers and nations, and over and above them, the question was posed in all its integral character in the Great War of 1914, and that in this sense European post-War society is still engaged in its new and gigantic struggle for existence and for its fate to this very day. *It is a transition of middle-class democracy from old to new forms and stages of a higher and at the same time more profound humanitarian democracy* in which all the classes and all the citizens are to receive their due place in the new harmonious entity of State and nations.

In giving the book in which he describes his activities during the War and interprets the philosophical, cultural, political, and social meaning of that war from the angle of history, the title of "The World Revolution" he desired to express this great truth and to indicate how he understood the development of the contemporary world and Europe.

And in an understanding of this development, of this gradual and peaceful linking up of our nation and our new State with it, Masaryk saw guarantees for the future of its present-day freedom and its lasting triumph.

What Europe is passing through to-day—this medley of dissensions, fights, revolutions and spiritual upheavals, this diversity of political and social regimes, of national and international movements, of moral and philosophical conflicts—all this constitutes the problem with which Masaryk occupied himself. It is his understanding of all this and his action in accordance with it that makes him great. Nothing of what we are passing through to-day surprised him, nothing found him unprepared mentally or morally or from the angle of learning or philosophy, nothing shook him, nothing forced him from his path of life—that path firm as steel and logically straight—up to the last moments that preceded his death.

Feudal society prior to the French Revolution was maintained in its social cohesion by the class order and class ideology, by the class authority of the aristocracy and the authority of the Church, underpropped by the political absolutism of the Monarchy. This pre-revolution social order was overthrown by revolutions, a Third Estate—that of the middle-class—was introduced to the struggle for a new order, and there was created a new system to which we give the name of middle-class civilisation and middle-class democracy.

But revolutionary political individualism and the philosophy of the rights of the man and citizen, having disintegrated feudal society and introduced a new social element into the structure of society—the middle-class—simultaneously with the raising of the fabric of a new order of middle-class civilisation and democracy, brought with them the germs of their own dissolution. The advancing application of the rights of man and citizen evoked in political life a *Fourth Estate* and posed the question of how to give *the broad masses of the people* a due share in the new social order. This raised the real problem of democracy, of a consistent popular government—not government by a class, by a party or by several classes, but government and administration by all, government and administration by the people, all the people.

The Fourth Estate demonstrated its political existence to the world in the revolution of the year 1848. In the course of the subsequent development of Europe and particularly in 1870 it took up a fighting attitude. From the Eighties onwards the farmer, the worker, the lower middle-class man sharply voices his claim for a share in the power, in co-government and in the new social order. Revolutionary individualism in its artistic and romantic literary form evoked among us the first investigation of the case of the humble individual in the spirit of social humanitarism and began to occupy itself with the Fourth Estate from the angle of art and literature: naturalism and realism in literature and art created the social and popular novel and an art of social tendencies. It cooperated in preparing the socialist political movement, the political democracy of the rural population and the democracy of the humble individual.

The second current of this revolutionary literary, artistic and philosophical individualism follows psychological lines: from Descartes, throughout the revolutions and finally under the romanticism of the nineteenth century man became the centre of all interest and all studies, of all the cares and all the joys of life. Modern psychology and psychologism, take asunder, dissect, analyse and study the individual, the man and the innermost aspects of *his soul*. Literary and artistic psychological analysis gives us modern symbolism and decadence, expressionism and estheticism, it investigates in merciless and brutal fashion the very innermost of man, discovers the passionate struggle of the rational and irrational in human personality, presents to us the gigantic conflicts of reason, passion, feeling, intellect, sensibility and sub-consciousness, creates that pre-War and post-War anarchistic subjectivism and that modern disorganised, restless, egocentric, egoistic individual in the whole scale of graduation from his assumption of the titan down to the sceptic, pusillanimous or cynical suicide.

Political and social development corresponds to this twofold intellectual and moral development in the sphere of thought, of literature and art: From 1848 onwards there developed political doctrines, movements and parties to uphold the interests and the rights of the workers; from the Seventies of last century the movement claimed the rural classes and the lower middle-classes; it would seem as if the cosmopolitan, pacifist and enlightened philosophy of the French Revolution led logically to international fraternization, to social equality, to a gradual application of political and social fraternity and humanity in the new democratic order based on equality. Parallel with development of these tendencies towards social justice and democratic equality there was, as their natural and necessary consequence, an inevitable and gradual emancipation of the oppressed and unfree nations of Europe, and an emphasis upon the national idea varying from romantic and sentimental patriotism to conscious national realism, on to the exaggerated nationalism of to-day.

This development did not, of course, halt at sentimental talk of social justice nor was it limited to appeals to the wealthier classes of society for more humanity. It took over the older conception of social class differences, elaborated a new doctrine of class struggle, it carried the social problem from the sphere of moral reflections to the field of scientific consideration, and in the struggle for a new social order emphasized more the material strength of the masses and their organisation than the power of the spirit and ethical reasons of humanity. We had now reached the epoch of scientific and class socialism of the Marxist order.

On the other hand disintegrating subjectivism—also an outcome of the French Revolution—began towards the close of the nineteenth century to spread to the political and social sphere. It sought the essence of the human being rather in instinct, passion and feeling than in man's intellectual and rational aspect, revolted against the rationalistic ideology of the French Revolution, did not believe in internationalism, nor in the brotherhood of man, did not believe in the thesis that in essence man is good and that human development and progress may proceed without wars, without bloody struggles and without violence. It erected its social and political theories upon the doctrine of human and simultaneously national egoism, upon the doctrine of the new authority of an anonymous collectivity of sentiment as opposed to the individual, and of that of the titanic individual against the anonymous mass sentiment, upon the doctrine of the impossibility, the failure of and crisis in rationalistic and intellectual democracy.

These movements too are popular movements, these doctrines too call for a new social order and they too include the Fourth Estate in the new social and political hierarchy. They do so indeed much more radically and ruthlessly than did post-War democracy. They choose, however, new methods; they do not believe in the democratic line of evolution, they lift collective discipline above the freedom of the individual, they lay upon the individual grave spiritual and material sacrifices, they demand of him unconditional devotion to the totality of the State, the nation and the party *as a new social authority* giving to all this a national and nationalist basis: the strength, the expansion, the honour and prestige of the nation and the national State which they raise to the rank of the absolute that decides on the future development of the world, the development of the world being determined by the rivalries and struggles between these great national entities.

This brings us to the end of one great heroic epoch that culminated in the Great War, which has brought present-day society to the parting of the ways, and which to-day presents us with a sharp and clear-cut dilemma: Will European society as an outcome of the French Revolution, after passing through the system of Liberalism in which it outlived itself and which it abandoned, develop—at least for a time—into what we call the extreme Right, or into what is currently known to-day as the extreme Left? Will it return, at least partially, to the creation of some new corporative or collective authority, personified in the leadership principle, so as to check the anarchistic instincts of the liberated individual and submit entirely to the State principle of totalitarianism, or will it continue to make efforts towards the unattainable ideals of absolute human equality, and thus in the end disembogue in a grave conflict between the two trends, and culminate in chaos and in catastrophe for the whole of modern civilisation?

Thus *a new vital problem of existence and fate* automatically presented itself to this post-revolution and post-War Europe: will this society of ours be able to check the revolutionary individualism of either side—whether of the rational or the irrational line? Will it be able to tell the modern liberated individual where the limits of his freedom run, so as to preserve for him the right measure of his real freedom and to prevent him being flung back into the chains of this or that slavery? Will it be able to create a new social authority which will be the cement, as it were, holding the new democratic society in cohesion? Will it be able to create a new democratic authority capable of taking the place of the former authority of the Monarchy, of the aristocracy and the Church, an authority that would mean a genuine harmony and synthesis of the rights and liberties of the individual with his duties to society and to his nation as an entity, an authority which will make the totalitarian doctrines superfluous on the one hand and will prevent the development of the unchained individual, after vain attempts at creating an ideal regime of absolute civic equality, from degenerating into moral, political and social anarchy and into complete economic chaos on the other?

And now we see before us the present-day chaos in Europe and the world—its philosophical and moral struggles, its political and social conflicts—and we see Masaryk as philosopher and statesman looking upon it all, looking down upon it all, calmly, firmly, in sovereign mien from the height of his eighty-seven years, taking it all in and passing judgment upon it.

Masaryk posed this problem very clearly to himself in the form, as we see it to-day, as early as the Nineties of last century. In his "Czech Question", "Our Present Crisis", "Social Question", "Modern Man and Religion", "Humanitarian Ideals", "Russia and Europe", and above all of course in his "World Revolution", he deals with it and substantially solves it. In his two books of "Talks"—with Karel Čapek and Emil Ludwig—and in several of his presidential speeches he returned to these questions. In the solution of this question I see the most dramatic moment in the intellectual development of Masaryk, just as I see the most dramatic moments of Masaryk's life in the year 1917 after the revolution in Moscow and all Russia, and in the early years of our own independent State. He pondered this problem up to the last few hours before he died; and he never for a moment faltered in its solution.

Masaryk gives this clear and unequivocal answer to the question: as philosopher, student of noetics, and metaphysician he does not say that we recognize the substance of things but only that we are continually drawing nearer and nearer to a knowledge of the absolute by way of the senses, reason, intuition and feeling. Equally as a student of ethics, as a sociologist and statesman Masaryk does not say that we are realizing the perfectly ideal State and the social happiness of all citizens from the angle of politics and society but only that by effective love of our fellow-men and by a politically just balance of the needs and interests of every kind and by collaboration among all we must daily draw ever nearer to that ideal.

As philosopher and metaphysician Masaryk saw in the individual, in man, a manifestation of the absolute and the most beautiful creation of Providence—something thus inviolate in his substance, in his spirituality and in metaphysical and ethical equality with the rest of mankind. His thought cannot be dissociated from the religious element. Man can therefore be only the *object* of thought, the *object* of political and social activity, *never an instrument or means*. Nor can the nation, nor may the nation, composed of people, of individuals thus respected, be an instrument or means; neither can it or may it be something above the individual, something to which the individual is sacrificed, something which as a collectivity is deified. The dignity of man suffices to become the basis of the dignity and strength of the nation. Nor is it possible to permit of such deification in the case of the State.

Man, the direct and real aim of all human political and social activity, creates jointly with others his human and national inviolable culture as an organic part of his being, and in harmony and in collaboration with all evolves a State and social organisation in which respect for his individuality is repaid by respect for the individuality of fellow-citizens, while at the same time his liberty is limited by respect for the liberty of others.

Such in content and methods is the sense of Masaryk's democracy. It is simple, just as every great truth is simple. Masaryk the democrat simply smooths out differences and draws extremes together by a never-halting evolution, driving the world ever higher and forward by force of thought, by practical activity and by applying the evolutionary method in political and social life. He seeks a synthesis of conflicts in the spheres of thought, of morals and daily life, he is a great balancer of arguments, sentiments and interests, accepts no extremes either from the Left or the Right—which, however, does not in his case mean the acceptance of mechanical eclecticism. He takes no step backwards into the past, but he indulges in no illusions about attempts at the ideal or conceptions however bold. He fought daily and incessantly for a better, juster and evolutionary more perfect society, for a more balanced, a morally riper and spiritually stronger man. That was his all-round *realism* in life and in philosophy.

You all know how he studied everything thoroughly and how he wrote on socialism and communism, on the crisis in Liberalism and the modern bourgeoisie, intelligentzia and middle-class democracy, on the development of the Church and religion, the fights he fought in the name of religion, faith in man and in his philosophic realism against decadence, aestheticism, the disintegrating aspects of modern subjectivism and suicidal scepticism, just as he fought against playing at false titanism and against absolutism of every kind. That in content and in method is the sense of his democracy. It is simple, just as every great truth is simple.

All these movements and trends of thought issued from revolutionary individualism and the post-revolution romanticism of the nineteenth century, and all of them in various forms manifest themselves in the chaotic Europe of to-day both in the realm of thought and in that of daily life.

You know, too, how all through his life he fought in his philosophical theories and in practical politics as philosopher, student of noetics and statesman for an equilibrium between sentiment and reason, how he refused to have anything to do with passionate and supersensitive nationalism, for he never based life and the world upon passions, feeling and instinct, as is done by numbers of post-War political and social systems. He saw clearly what a bloody struggle and what individual and collective violence, what chaos and errant thought in the moral, political and social—in the internal as well as in the international political sphere—would dominate Europe if instinct and the primitivism of feeling should gain the upper hand in a struggle among the States and nations.

After a long life of painstaking thought, after a long and responsible career of practical affairs, he turned to the fountain of his unique life-experiences and expressed quietly, firmly, platonically and in a Christian spirit, his answer to all these questions of the disturbed Europe of to-day in a formula which was simultaneously his philosophy and life's practice and which in strikingly expressive manner contrasted in all their historical greatness two great moral worlds that oppose one another: *Jesus—not Caesar.*

From the angle of philosophy he summed up this whole faith of his, this philosophy of history and practical policy of balanced, steadfast, clear-sighted man in these lapidary, eternally valid words:

"The profoundest argument for democracy is faith in man, in his worth, in his intellect and immortal soul; this is true metaphysical equality. From the ethical angle democracy is justified as a political realisation of love of one's fellow-men. Things that are eternal cannot be matters of indifference to an immortal, the immortal cannot abuse the immortal, cannot exploit it, or do it violence. True democracy, based upon love and respect to one's fellow-men, and to all that are near is the realization of the divine order upon earth."

This is another formula for humanity and democracy not merely as regards content but also method of work and of the bringing about by evolution of a new world and leading the world of to-day from its maze of error.

Humanitarian democracy as a cultural, social and political system is for Masaryk no mere theory, system of thought and theses or schematic institutions. Nor is it for him a question of dispute as to whether it will come or not, whether it will maintain itself or not. It is a moral, political and social regime and status given by the historical-philosophical evolution of the modern world, a regime and status that events may hold up, that other systems may for a while supplant—but the evolution goes irresistibly on, humanitarian democracy comes, and will come in all fulness.

To be a democrat meant for Masaryk to create a logically balanced synthesis of all man's spiritual powers, a balance and inner discipline of soul, an equilibrium of intellect and feeling, the heroic conscious strength of the human self, and at the same time pious humility in the face of the world and its metaphysical problem, before man in his millions of masks, and before the right of every one of mankind to happiness and a genuinely human, free existence. It is a great positive factor of the human soul, an emphasis on and positive attitude towards every problem of life, to every personality, to every class, to every nation, to the whole problem of the external world. It is a resistance to all violence whether spiritual or material, and thus the right and resultant determination to defend oneself against violence.

Masaryk's life was a great struggle with his own ego for inner balance, clarity, firmness, a struggle with the external world and its problems for a full and positive comprehension of that world, a struggle *against all negativism and for full harmony* between the individual and the world, for the full life of man *sub specie aeternitas*.

All this Masaryk desired to be, and such he was.

Masaryk's life reached its culmination point in the Great War which to-day appears to us as the final point of the development of Europe from the Napoleonic wars down to 1914; as the definitive collapse of aristocratism and theocratism in its mediaeval form, as an attempt to solve the social problem in its modern democratic form, as a definitive emancipation of the small European nations and their introduction to collaboration among the European and world powers in ensuring universal peace. We have seen what a vast volume of philosophical, moral, political and social problems covering the whole nineteenth and beginning of the twentieth century Masaryk mastered, reflected upon, and solved for himself; we know what political experience he possessed in his sixty-fifth year at the moment when the War broke out. Few persons were at that moment so well prepared for warlike events of world import as was Masaryk.

At a moment when his spiritual evolution had attained its balance and fulness, and when he was almost prepared to bring his career to a close, this moralist and philosopher suddenly found himself face to face with problems of the most fateful nature for a man of morality and a statesman: He found himself face to face with the question of the use of force, and that, too, of force en masse, face to face with a great and fateful war. As a politician who all his life had pondered the fortunes of his nation and had formulated in such expressive fashion the philosophy of Czech history, he found himself suddenly faced with unexpected eventualities: with the possibility of the collapse of the Austro-Hungarian Monarchy, or the possibility of the triumph of the two Central Powers over the rest of Europe, with the possibility of a great victory for his own nation or the possibility of its further and more perilous existence in a post-War Europe that would be dominated by the two former dynasties. Seldom has a responsible politician ever been faced with a decision more far-reaching, more fateful, more dramatic for his nation, for its whole future and for its whole history.

Even then he dominated these terrible and fateful problems of war. First of all he solved the moral problem of war, the moral problem of revolution and of political and military revolt for himself alone. He examined the question of what war, revolution and revolt would mean for the nation from the moral, cultural, political and social standpoints. He solved the moral problem of the organisation of a revolutionary army, made his plan of political action, and at sixty-five left his native land for a task the greatness, the extent, and the responsibility of which then surpassed all our imagination. The leading motive of his decision was not merely the sense of duty for a politician to be at his post in the decisive moment of his nation's history but first and foremost a *moral duty:* that it was essential at all costs to take a stand against the possible triumph of a moral evil and against the triumph of a policy that would result in other great and terrible wars.

From home he took with him to the Allied countries a knowledge of the political and military problems of the Central European countries and of Russia. During his sojourn in the Allied countries during the War he thoroughly studied and made himself acquainted with the political, diplomatic and military aims and possibilities of the Allies. Hence arose his well-known political plan and practical programme for the war and its outcome. He incorporated this in his study on "The New Europe". In that work he outlined a programme of the War and the peace to follow it, propounded in it his wartime and peacetime credo, forecasted clearly our future State with its political, social, economic and nationality problems. This plan and this practical programme, too, corresponded to his life's ideals of humanity, his morality and his principles of justice.

In a manner rare in the annals of the nations he became, at the head of a victorious legionary army, the triumphant leader of a nation fighting for its liberty; he restored to life an old State with its thousand years of tradition, and to it united by common effort the Slovak branch of the nation. He returned from exile as the President of this State and became President-Liberator. It is rightly said that seldom has a man issuing from the humblest ranks and from a small nation attained to such dizzy heights of world doings, of decisions deciding the fate of the world, of international triumph and of national and State apotheosis as Masaryk. To-day, at the moment when he is leaving us for ever, we see that this is not merely national and State triumph and recognition. It is world recognition.

As President of the restored State he had one more great satisfaction in his great life. He lived for nearly 19 years more after the achievement of his triumph, he placed himself at the service of his nation and State with his faith, his wisdom, his experience, and his iron will, at a time that still suffered gravely from the War and its effects; with his fellow-workers he built up day by day according to his own ideas, according to the development of Europe and the world, according to his assessment of our own forces and those around us, our system of democracy, our internal administration, our economic system, our army, our foreign policy, and thus linked up our new existence and State with the new post-War system of Europe, and with the other nations of the world.

He saw the actual success of this great pioneer work and he was a happy and successful man also in his passing, for he went away in the firm faith that the structure which he had built was upon firm foundations, that we all jointly rule it, and that our State and all our citizens of all classes and nationalities are, and will be, competent for their task.

How are we to mourn over this great life in its passing when we look upon that splendid, perfect circle of existence, which of its very self is a great call to indomitable faith in the good, the positive, in success, in beneficent moral development rising to the highest points; a life which of itself in the moment of its passing is the personification of harmony itself! How beautiful and how exalting is it to see that this great warrior, who never shirked a fight, leaves us at a moment of grevious problems and of struggles in the whole world, leaves us in harmony with himself, with his faith in Providence, in harmony with his environment, with his faith in man, faith in the ultimate triumph of man, in the triumph of justice and truth, in the triumph of humanity here amongst us, in Europe and throughout the world!

In that firm faith in a happy future and in that striving for harmony of personal, national and State life he is our pattern for the work that lies before us. He will be the symbol of our evolutionary harmony of class and social elements, the symbol of ever renewing harmony of persons and parties, the symbol of harmony among the nationalities in our State. He is, and always will be for us, a great call to keep on seeking paths by which we may unite in the name of humanity and democracy for the common effort to which our lot claims us all in this State.

I call upon you all without exception, from Left to Right, from the remotest hamlet to this our metropolis, from Aš to Jasiňa—I call upon all of you who ponder most upon the social problems of this State and upon you who devote your attention most to nationality problems—*I call upon all of you without distinction, in the spirit and in the remembrance of our First President, to take up your heritage from him and complete his work, the perfecting of our just, firm, indomitable, evolutionary, humanitarian democracy.*

Though he passes, Masaryk is still amongst us; he is the model and the call for each one of us. He is the model of great faith in man, of which there is to-day such need in Europe and throughout the world: the call for us to be harmonious among ourselves, in good will and in friendship with our neighbours and the other countries of Europe and of the world to build up our State organism and our political, social and nationality collaboration in such manner that we may make of this our place in Europe a perfect and harmonious State, just in its social, nationality and political system, a State that shall be worthy of him who has just left us, *a State that shall be among the States what Masaryk was amongst us, and what Masaryk was to the rest of the world.*

This call means that we must remain faithful to Masaryk. In bidding him farewell in your name I promise that we shall obey the call.

President Liberator, we will remain faithful to the heritage which you have laid in our hands!

Dr. Edvard Beneš
MASARYK'S PATH AND LEGACY
Funeral oration at the burial of the President-Liberator 21. September 1937

This booklet is issued in a limited edition of 1000 copies. Drawings and reproduction of a wooden engraving by Karel Svolinský. Printed by the Orbis works with Egmont and Menhart types, Prague, October 1937

Publishers' Note:

The text of the Speech of President Dr. Edvard Beneš is printed from the original manuscript and contains those portions which, owing to the necessity of shortening the time of delivery, were omitted on the occasion of the funeral ceremony itself. In the view of this, the text which appeared in the daily press has in a number of places undergone some few changes.